Next Stop

MARS

By Judy Nayer

Modern Curriculum Press
Parsippany, New Jersey

Credits

Photos: All photos © Pearson Learning unless otherwise noted.
Cover & title page: NASA. 5: U.S. Geological Survey/Science Photo Library/Photo
Researchers, Inc. 7: U.S. Geological Survey, Flagstaff Arizona/NASA. 8: U.S.
Geological Survey/Science Photo Library/Photo Researchers, Inc. 10: Inset: Lowell
Observatory. 10: Lowell Observatory. 11: David A. Hardy/Science Photo
Library/Photo Researchers, Inc. 12: California Institute of Technology & Hale
Observatories. 13: NASA/JPL/Caltech. 14-15: NASA/JPL/Caltech. 16: David A.
Hardy/Science Photo Library/Photo Researchers, Inc. 17: NASA. 18: U.S. Geological
Survey, Flagstaff Arizona/NASA. 19: Martin Marietta Corp. 20: A.S.P./Science
Source/Photo Researchers, Inc. 21: Sojouner Mars Rover and spacecraft design and
images ©1996-1997, California Institute of Technology all rights reserved. 22:
NASA/JPL/Caltech. 23: NASA. Unit Opener Borders: Space Telescope Science
Institute.

Cover by Lisa Arcuri

Book design by Stephen Barth

Modern Curriculum Press
An imprint of Pearson Learning
299 Jefferson Road, P.O. Box 480
Parsippany, NJ 07054–0480

www.pearsonlearning.com

1-800-321-3106

ISBN 0-7652-1374-5

2 3 4 5 6 7 8 9 10 UP 08 07 06 05 04 03 02 01 00

Modern
Curriculum
Press

Contents

To those who risked their lives
to explore space

Chapter 1
Neighbors in Space

On a clear night, look up at the sky. Look for a glowing red dot. It is not a star. It is a planet called Mars.

Mars

A planet can be made of dirt, rock, and sometimes gas. There are nine planets that travel around our Sun. Our Earth is the third planet from the Sun. Mars is the fourth planet, right after Earth. Mars and Earth are next-door neighbors!

Our solar system has nine planets.

Mars is drier than Earth.

Mars is different from Earth. It is only about half the size. If you look at Mars through a telescope, the planet looks reddish. It is much colder than Earth. The temperatures are almost always below zero. The air is so thin a person could not breathe it. Still, Mars is the planet most like Earth.

Mars is like Earth in many ways. It has days and nights. There are ice caps at the top and bottom. Both planets also have moons. Earth has one moon. Mars has two.

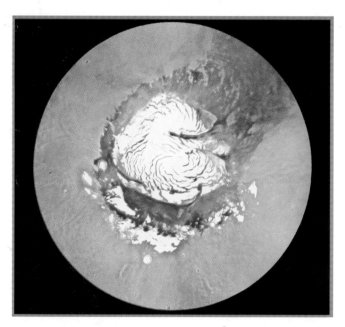

Ice cap on Mars

Mars Up Close

Mars has many dust storms. Some dust storms on Mars can last for months.

Chapter 2
Life on Mars?

For a long time, people thought Mars was even more like Earth. They thought there was life on Mars.

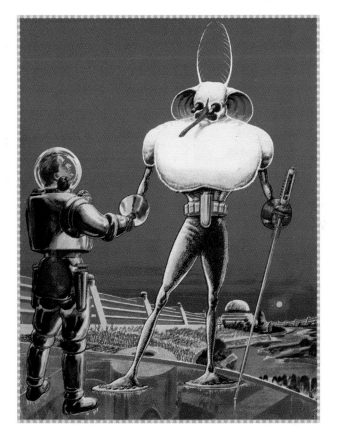

An artist's idea of what a Martian might look like

About 100 years ago a scientist looked at Mars through a telescope. He saw dark lines on the planet. He thought they were canals. Canals are like small rivers. People build canals on Earth to carry water.

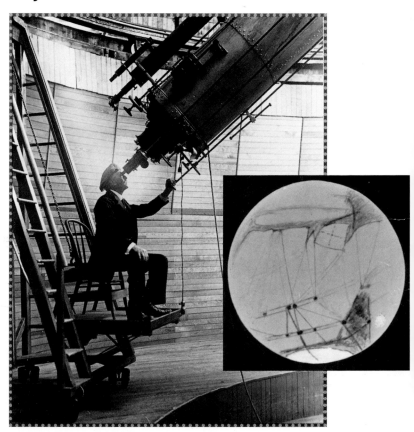

Percival Lowell drew what he saw on Mars. He thought the lines were canals.

A Martian city in a story

People began to say that the canals were built by Martians. They imagined that Martians lived on Mars in cities like ours. Then people began to make up stories about Martians. Some stories were about little green people in flying saucers. Some were about unfriendly creatures who attacked Earth.

Scientists did not know if there was life on Mars. They could not see enough of the planet through their telescopes. So they built a spacecraft to go to Mars.

Hale telescope at Mount Palomar Observatory

Mars Up Close

Today a small spacecraft takes six months to get to Mars.

Chapter 3
Pictures of Mars

The first spacecraft to visit Mars was Mariner 4 in 1965. It had special cameras. It got close enough to take pictures of Mars. Then it sent the pictures back to Earth.

Mariner 4

The surface of Mars is rocky and dry.

The people who saw the pictures were disappointed. There were no canals, no cities, and no Martians. There were no plants or animals. There were no signs of life at all.

The pictures did show a rocky desert. The rocks and soil may look red because they have a lot of iron in them. Blowing wind picks up the dust. The dust in the air makes the sky look red or pink.

In 1971 scientists sent another spacecraft to Mars. This one went around the planet. It took lots of pictures. They showed no signs of life. Yet, there were many new discoveries.

Mariner 9

Mars Up Close

Mars may not be as red as people think. New cameras show pictures of a yellow-brown planet.

Chapter 4
New Discoveries

What did the 1971 spacecraft see on Mars? It found four huge volcanoes. A volcano is a mountain that spits out fire and liquid rock. One volcano is the biggest volcano anyone has ever seen. It is over 15 miles high!

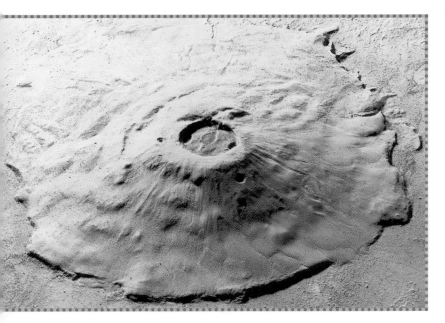

Olympus Mons volcano on Mars

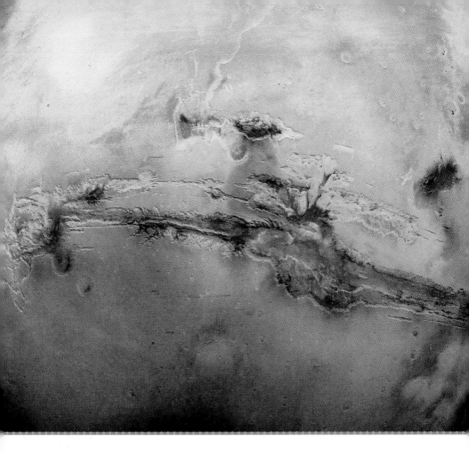

A giant canyon on Mars

Mars also has giant canyons. The biggest is ten times longer and three times deeper than the Grand Canyon on Earth. It is so big that it could stretch all the way across the United States.

In 1976 two spacecraft landed on Mars. They sent back the first pictures from the ground. These pictures showed the biggest discovery of all. They showed long, deep grooves, or cuts, in the ground.

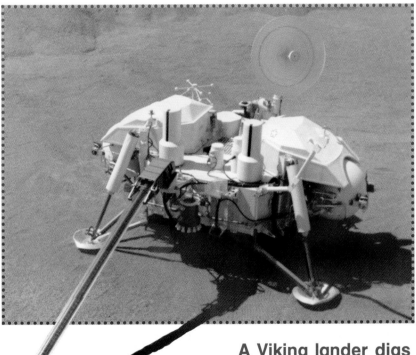

A Viking lander digs in the Martian soil.

Scientists think the grooves were made by flowing water. Long ago Mars may have been warmer and wetter. Simple forms of life may have lived on Mars then.

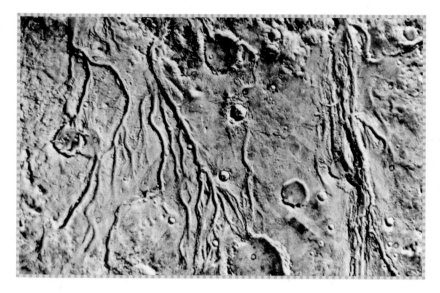

Dry channels may have been made by flowing water.

Mars Up Close

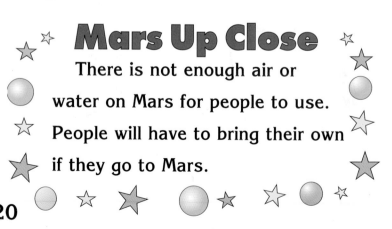

There is not enough air or water on Mars for people to use. People will have to bring their own if they go to Mars.

Chapter 5
Exploring Mars

In 1997 a spacecraft called the *Pathfinder* landed on Mars. On the spacecraft was a little robot called *Sojourner*. With a computer, scientists on Earth made *Sojourner* move around on Mars. The robot ran on wheels like a remote-control car.

The word *sojourner* means "someone who stays for a little while."

Scientists named this rock Yogi.

Pathfinder studied temperature and wind speed. *Sojourner* looked at rocks and dirt. It found rocks shaped long ago by wind and water.

Scientists plan to send more spacecraft to Mars. Some will have robot arms that will dig into the ground to look for water. Others will bring dirt and rocks back to Earth.

Someday, people may go to Mars. Maybe you will be able to watch when the first people set foot on Mars. Maybe you will be one of those visitors to our neighbor in space.

People may one day live on Mars.

Mars Up Close

Because Mars is smaller than Earth, things weigh less on Mars. A 100-pound person would weigh only 38 pounds on Mars.

Glossary

canyon   [KAN yun] a narrow valley with high, steep sides

computer   [kum PYOO tur] a machine that stores and works with facts or information

planet   [PLAN ut] one of the bodies, like Earth, that moves around the Sun

remote-control   [ree MOHT kun TROHL] being controlled by an object from a distance

robot   [ROH baht] a machine that does work people tell it to do

scientist   [SYE un tihst] a person who studies a science, or facts about the physical world

spacecraft   [SPAYS kraft] a spaceship or any object made to be used in outer space

telescope   [TEL uh skohp] an instrument for looking at faraway objects